Cryptocurrency:

*Beginner's Simplified
Guide
to Make Money
with Cryptocurrency*

Gavin S. Finney

Table of Contents

Introduction

Chapter 1: What is Cryptocurrency?

Chapter 2: Why Cryptocurrency Can Be a Good Investment

Chapter 3: How Cryptocurrency Works

Chapter 4: The Cryptocurrency Blockchain

Chapter 5: Different Cryptocurrencies and Picking the Right One

Chapter 6: Making your first Cryptocurrency Transaction

Chapter 7: Storing Cryptocurrencies

Chapter 8: Investing in Cryptocurrency

Chapter 9: How to Avoid Investing Mistakes in Cryptocurrency

Chapter 10: Trading in Cryptocurrency

Chapter 11: Risk Management Essentials for Cryptocurrency Investing

Bonus Chapter: Cryptocurrency Mining Essentials – The Benefits and How It Works

Conclusion

About the Author

What This Book Will Teach You

Are you curious to learn about making money from Cryptocurrency but unsure where to start?

Have you always wanted to learn more about Cryptocurrency, but are intimidated by the technical jargon being used?

If these questions relate well with you, then this book is for you. In this book, you will find the basic essentials to learning about Cryptocurrency. This book introduces readers to the investing side of Cryptocurrency, the in's and out, the various processes and steps involved in it.

Who this Book is for

This book contains information on how to learn about Cryptocurrency from a beginner level.

Readers who can benefit the most from the book include:

- Individuals interested in making money from Cryptocurrency

- Investing enthusiasts who want to learn about Cryptocurrency as another possible source of income

- Readers who would like to know information about Cryptocurrency

How this Book is Organized

This book is organized into three parts. The parts are best read in chronological order. Once you become familiar with all the steps outlined in the book, you can go directly to the techniques which apply to your current situation the best.

The three parts of the book are:

Part One outlines the essential topics on

Cryptocurrency. The section also talks about how important it is to learn these topics as a beginner in order to form a solid foundation in doing the right steps – from introductory concepts to making your first Cryptocurrency transaction.

Part Two is about the Investing and Trading side of Cryptocurrency and what investing mistakes you can avoid in order to help minimize the chances of you losing your money. You'll learn how the process works and how to implement the steps discussed.

Part Three are the other important topics on Cryptocurrency such as:

- Risk Management Essentials

- Cryptocurrency Mining Essentials

After each chapter, you will be provided with lessons and exercises in order to leverage the information found on this book.

By reading and implementing the steps outlined on this book, you will be able to understand Cryptocurrency essentials in helping you achieve your money-making goals.

Introduction:

If you're new to the world of Cryptocurrency, it can be a minefield of baffling terminology and concepts that can be tricky to get your head around. Interest in cryptocurrency has grown quickly over the past few years. This is due mostly to the incredible success of Bitcoin, the first cryptocurrency to be introduced to the market. Due to the enormous increases in Bitcoin values, many people have become interested in buying cryptocurrencies as an investment opportunity. In this guide, we will help you to understand in simple terms, what cryptocurrencies are and how they work. You will learn:

- Why cryptocurrency can be a good investment
- What the technical jargon means
- How to make a cryptocurrency transaction
- How cryptocurrency is stored

- How to make investments in cryptocurrency
- How to avoid making rookie mistakes

New cryptocurrencies are being launched onto the marketplace daily, and it would seem they are here to stay. Over time, it's predicted they will become commonplace in everyday financial transactions of all types. It can therefore only be beneficial to understand them. Welcome to the future of money. Shall we begin?

Chapter 1:
What is
Cryptocurrency?

CRYPTO **COINS**

Chapter 1: What is Cryptocurrency?

The definition of the word Cryptocurrency is:

A digital currency where encryption coding is used to determine and regulate the creation of currency units and also to verify the electronic transfer of funds. It operates outside the remit of any bank.

The idea behind Cryptocurrency was to create a form of exchangeable and tradable currency that could be used online between two people without the need for a third party such as a bank.

The word "Cryptocurrency" was first coined by a member of the "Bitcoin Forum," it was liked by the developers of Bitcoin and brought into general use.

The History of Cryptocurrency

1998 to 2009 before Bitcoin

Before Bitcoin, which was the first

cryptocurrency to be fully established, there were attempts at creating other ideas for digital currencies that were secured with encryption.

Internet commerce was beginning to expand exponentially. In order for electronic payments to be made, it was necessary to use a third party financial institution such as a bank, credit card company or service like PayPal. For most transactions, this is fine, but it can carry additional costs and risks. The transaction can be reversed or blocked. In the non-digital world, physical currency, money or Fiat money as it is correctly called, can be used to pay for goods and services. This means no middleman is involved. But in the digital world, this simply wasn't possible.

An electronic payment method that was based on cryptographic proof rather than trust, which allowed two parties to make transactions directly with one another was needed. It was necessary to ensure that these transactions, once made, were not possible to reverse and could protect the seller from fraudulent activity, while also giving the buyer protection.

B-money was the first proposal. It was created by Wei Dai, an American computer engineer who worked at the Microsoft Corporation in Redmond, Washington in cryptography research. Shortly after, Nick Szabo, a computer scientist and cryptographer, proposed another system called Bit Gold. Although neither proposal was formally adopted, the fundamental ideas were used in the creation of the first cryptocurrency, bitcoin.

2008 to 2009 – The Evolution of Bitcoin

The domain name bitcoin.org was first registered on the 18 August 2008.

On the 31 October 2008, a paper called "Bitcoin: A Peer to Peer Electronic Cash System," was posted to a discussion mailing list on the subject of cryptography. The authors of this paper called themselves Satoshi Nakamoto, but the true identity of this person or persons is still not truly known.

In January 2009, the Bitcoin network was born, when Satoshi first made the software available to members of the general public. The software allowed anyone who downloaded it to obtain free bitcoins in a bid to encourage people to become interested in the idea. Satoshi was the first to mine a block of bitcoins. This block was known as "The Genesis Block" and had a reward of 50 bitcoins.

Initially, the idea didn't take off, as anyone at the time was interested in the concept. This, however, was about to change, when Martti Malmi - also known as Sirius - a reclusive student at the Helsinki University of Technology in Finland, discovered the Bitcoin.org website and became interested in the idea behind it. In May 2009, Martti emailed Satoshi, offering his services to further develop Bitcoin. Within a few weeks of this initial contact, the Bitcoin website had been totally revamped using Martti's ideas. He then went on to teach himself the C++ code that Satoshi had used to write Bitcoin. Soon Martti became the main developer of Bitcoin and created the Bitcoin forum. A member of the forum used the term Cryptocurrency in a post and Satoshi, and Martti liked it so much that they went on to use it.

Hal Finney, a video game developer who graduated from Caltech with a degree in engineering in 1981, was also a supporter of bitcoin. He downloaded the software on the first day of its release, receiving 10 bitcoins in return. This was the world's first ever bitcoin transaction.

It's estimated that Satoshi mined around 1 million bitcoins prior to giving up his involvement.

2010 – Bitcoin gains a value

At this point bitcoins had not been traded, they had only been mined. This meant it wasn't possible to give them any sort of monetary exchange value. This was until an individual decided to use his bitcoins to purchase two pizzas. He swapped 10,000 bitcoins in the transaction, which at today's value makes those two pizzas probably the most expensive take-out meal ever

A major problem with Bitcoin was discovered on 6 August 2010, when it was shown that some transactions had not been correctly verified prior to entry into the transaction log (blockchain). This meant users could effectively bypass the restrictions on how many bitcoins could be generated. This lead to the creation of over 184 billion being made by two addresses shown on the network. The transaction was quickly spotted and removed from the logs and the problem fixed. It is the only problem that has ever been experienced in bitcoin's history.

2011 - 2012 – The emergence of other cryptocurrencies

Following on from the growing popularity of Bitcoin, other cryptocurrencies began to appear. Litecoin and Namecoin are two examples. These new cryptocurrencies were often aimed at improving upon the Bitcoin, by promising faster speeds, greater encryption and other advantages. These currencies often referred to as altcoin (alternative to Bitcoin) now number in excess of 1000, and the number is only likely to rise as time goes on.

During this time Bitcoin continued to release new versions of their software, which they had now named Bitcoin Core

2013 – The crash of Bitcoin values.

Bitcoin reaches a price in excess of $1,000 per coin. A few days later China declares that Chinese banks and other financial institutions cannot accept bitcoins. The reason for this was that they didn't recognize a currency without legal status and felt that such currency should not be circulated. This caused panic in the market, with people fearing that other countries may follow suit. The price of a Bitcoin plummeted, and it took in excess of two years for it to recover back to its pre-crash value.

The Bitcoin site was updated into its current format with the addition of many new pages and the adding of extra software. The translation system was also created to make the site more accessible to people around the world.

2014 – Illegal activity

To facilitate the easy exchange of bitcoins many people use a bitcoin exchange. This is a digital marketplace that brings together buyers and sellers. These exchanges are usually recognized as being the safest places to trade bitcoins for other fiat currencies ($, £, €). It is a totally online platform which is used as an intermediary between potential buyers and sellers. The recognized abbreviation for bitcoin currency is BTC or XBT.

In January 2014, one of the world's then largest bitcoin exchanges called MT Gox suddenly disappeared overnight. At the time 850,000 bitcoins were being traded, and the owners of these bitcoins lost them forever. The investigation behind this is ongoing but the story behind exactly what happened that day is still something of a mystery. Whatever that story is, someone stole bitcoins that were then valued at $450 million dollars. Today they would be worth closer to $4.5 billion.

2016 – The arrival of Ethereum and ICOs.

The only other cryptocurrency to come close to the success of Bitcoin to date is Ethereum. That operates using a platform called Ether. Almost simultaneously Initial Coin Offerings or ICO's appeared on fundraising platforms. They offer investors the opportunity to trade in start-up ventures, often in the form of stocks and shares, in exactly the same way they can invest and trade in cryptocurrency. This is seen as being a dangerous investment, as ICO's can be scams set up by criminals to look like legitimate investments. Due to this, the Chinese government banned them completely.

2017 and beyond – The continued growth and popularity of Cryptocurrency

Over time, spending your Bitcoins has become easier, as the number of places that accepts them as a tradable currency continues to grow. It is anticipated that other cryptocurrencies will also become accepted as a form of legal tender and eventually you will be able to spend them down at your local store.

Many banking organizations, particularly those based in Europe are now looking at ways they could become involved with the trade in cryptocurrencies. They have seen what a huge market it is and understandably want their own slice of the pie.

They have been described as many things, ranging from the future of currency to a complete scam, but whatever you think of cryptocurrencies it would seem that they are most definitely here to stay. Some people even think they will replace money as we know it.

There are many different uses for the cryptocurrency, although to date only Bitcoin and Ethereum are really recognized widely. To give you some ideas of what you can do with your coins, here are some examples:

- Donate to charity and know that the full amount you send will be the amount they receive
- Travel the world and purchase all the extras, including flights, hotels, car rentals or even cruises
- Buy precious metals such as Gold or Platinum
- Buy or sell luxury items, from artwork to jewelry

- Get your kids a University education
- Use a Bitcoin ATM to withdraw money from your Bitcoin virtual money wallet
- Use Bitpay at a growing number of shops and online retailers to pay for just about anything from a coffee to a luxury yacht

You may wonder how it can be possible to pay for a coffee with Bitcoin when the value of a single Bitcoin is worth so much more. The beauty of cryptocurrency is that unlike regular money you don't just have to spend it by its single unit value. You can spend just a tiny part of a single coin's value because it's digital money.

For now, cryptocurrencies are really being used as investment and trading opportunities. If you had been lucky enough to purchase a single bitcoin when they were first launched, that coin would have been worth $0.008 at the time of writing that same bitcoin is now worth $14488.20. That means if you had invested just $8 dollars to buy 1000 bitcoins they would now be worth a staggering $14,488,200, yes you read that right; fourteen million, four hundred and eighty-eight thousand, two hundred dollars! Don't you just wish you'd invested in a few? We will focus on investments more closely, later on in the guide.

By giving yourself a basic understanding of the complexities of cryptocurrency and how it works, you'll be able to make the best choices when it comes to making wise investments into them.

When you've finished reading this guide on Cryptocurrencies, you will:

- Understand what cryptocurrencies are
- Know why they can be a good investment
- Understand how they work
- Know what a blockchain is
- Know which cryptocurrencies are available and how to pick the right one
- Understand how to perform a transaction
- Know how to store cryptocurrency

- Understand how to make investments in your chosen cryptocurrency
- Know how to avoid making investment mistakes
- Understand Cryptocurrency trading
- Know what mining means and how it works
- Understand all the main cryptocurrency jargon

A cryptocurrency transaction is quite a complex thing to understand, and here I have tried to break it down into its most basic components, we will look at everything in more detail as we go through the book:

- A transaction is when funds are moved from one digital wallet to another. A bit like transferring money from one bank account to another, only there is no third-party bank involved. The money goes directly from one wallet to the other.
- In order for crypto coins to be moved between wallets, for security they use an encrypted electronic signature. The

transaction is then verified and stored onto the public ledger, which holds all the transaction information.

Chapter Summary:

1. Cryptocurrency is a digital currency that uses complex encryption coding to regulate its creation.

2. It can be traded, and some can be used to purchase goods and services either online or in shops.

3. The first cryptocurrency was Bitcoin. It remains the most important and influential cryptocurrency today. Many other cryptocurrencies are now available.

4. Just like any other form of currency, cryptocurrencies are also prone to fraud and theft.

5. A cryptocurrency transaction is when coins are moved between two digital wallets using powerful encryption systems.

Your Quick Start Action Step:

Visit the website Forbes.com to find out more about the essentials of cryptocurrency.

Chapter 2: Why Cryptocurrency Can Be a Good Investment

Chapter 2: Why Cryptocurrency can be a Good Investment

What is investing within the context of Digital Currency and Cryptocurrency?

Cryptocurrency, as with any other type of investment, foreign currency, precious metals, stocks, and shares, is an asset that can be purchased or acquired, with the potential for growth in value over time.

As a long-term investment, cryptocurrency can be beneficial. This is so long as you are prepared to hold onto your investment long term. If you want the potential to earn a return on your money in the short term, trading will be a better way to cash in. Trading is a way of gaining regular, but smaller returns. Please see chapter 10 for more information.

Cryptocurrency can conceivably be thought of in a similar way to any other currency (fiat money), with which we are all familiar. This means it can be treated in the same way as using one currency to buy another, for example, Yen can be exchanged for Dollars, Pounds for Euros or Rupees for Rand and so on.

Exchange rates fluctuate, and the same is true in the world of cryptocurrency. One of the big differences within digital currencies, due largely to them still being relatively new to the investment scene, means their value has been quite volatile. This means that there are frequently huge gains and equally huge losses. These large fluctuations in unit values, when compared with the more mainstream forms of currency, are a lot more dramatic. But this is also what makes them so interesting.

Digital currency and cryptocurrency are not necessarily for the investor who's looking for a guaranteed return on investment. However, as with any good investment opportunity (in which there are always risks), it can provide some exciting opportunities. This is because it has been shown to have the ability to achieve incredible levels of growth in a very short time.

This is probably due to it still being very much in its infancy and like other currencies, once it became more mainstream and established it is likely to settle at much lower growth levels. This is why investment now when it is still so new, is such a great opportunity.

Building a basic foundation

Before blindly jumping on the cryptocurrency investment bandwagon, it's a good idea to research as extensively as you can, the many different options available. As with any investment, it's important to maintain a watchful eye on the market. Be prepared and plan in advance what you will do should the price fluctuate either in your favor or against it. There are also tax implications and brokerage fees to be considered if a brokerage acts on your behalf (which I would recommend). This is no different to any other type of investment opportunity.

There are many cryptocurrency exchanges, as there are traditional stock brokerages. While on the surface many will seem to be very similar in their fee structure and list of services they offer, it's a good idea to research, which one will best serve your needs. In order to do this, identifying exactly what it is you're going to want to do in advance is essential. You will need to decide:

- Whether it is one or many cryptocurrencies that you wish to trade in
- The level of exposure you want to any given cryptocurrency
- The long-term goals of your investment
- The short-term goals of your investment
- The ease of usage
- The amount of money you are happy to speculate

When choosing a broker, you will need to look at:

- Their fees
- Their guarantees
- The services that they offer
- Their payment options

How basic cryptocurrency investing is done

If you decide adding cryptocurrency elements to your investment portfolio is a good option for you, these are the first things you should do:

- Ask the questions 'Can I afford to invest? Can I afford not to?'
- Decide upon an initial investment level
- Find a brokerage that trades in the cryptocurrency of your choice

The following steps will help you to succeed when venturing into this field:

1. Sign up for an Exchange

In order to buy and or sell something, you need a marketplace. Cryptocurrency exchanges or brokers provide this for you. At the moment, 'Coinbase' is one of the most trusted exchanges. Although, at the time of writing, this investment opportunity is largely unregulated. Regulation is being discussed in all countries of the world. Coinbase is insured, giving you the security of your investment transactions being covered. This means if your own digital security is compromised you won't be out of pocket.

There are plenty of other options too, including Kraken, Cex.io, ShapeShift, Poloniex, Bitstamp, CoinMama, Bitsquare, LocalBitcoin, and Gemini. These are only a few examples, and there are many more. Some allow to you purchase your cryptocurrency with a debit or credit card or by bank transfer, while others only permit one type of cryptocurrency to be traded for another.

2. Security

Ensure you use really strong passwords. Get creative with the use of not only upper and lowercase characters but also numbers and symbols. Use "Two-Factor Authentication" such as Google Authenticator. This is a safer option than merely using a texted code, as the text could be misdirected by criminals. Coinbase uses two-factor authentication.

3. Invest in what you know.

Research, research, and more research. Your co-worker may well be right on his investment advice. However, it is far wiser to do your own research. There are plenty of forums where you can pick up the latest tips or research a cryptocurrency you are interested in. Take a look at the movements, and trending currencies on sites like coinmarketcap.com to get an idea of what is going on in the market right now.

4. Type of Trading

Long or Short term? Well, that all depends on you and what you are comfortable with and what you have the time for.

Some short-term options to look into include: Margin Trading, Futures Market, Binary Options Trading, Prediction Markets, Short-selling Bitcoin Assets or Day Trading.

Long-term trading is more about holding onto the currency for a prolonged period. Very few cryptocurrencies will enjoy the same success as Bitcoin, but if you do your homework, you should be able to find ones that will give you a good return if you keep hold of them for long enough.

5. Understand Bitcoin's Influence in the Market

Like the U.S. dollar is to the global economy, Bitcoin is to the cryptocurrencies of the world. When purchasing other cryptocurrencies, it is often Bitcoins that will be used to make that transaction. When trading in cryptocurrency, it's advisable to cross-reference them with bitcoin's charts, as a benchmark to see if there are any patterns developing.

6. Fluctuation in value

Try to think about the longer term. You are aiming for a gradual, steady, increase in value. For this to occur, patience is essential. Try not to panic about fluctuations in the price of a coin, and these storms should be weathered. If you hold your nerve, the likelihood is that the currency will rise again to higher levels.

7. Use the experts

Seek out expert advice. Experts can help you make better-informed choices, they may cost you a little at the outset, but in the long term, their advice could prove invaluable.

8. Taxes

Cryptocurrency is currently classified, by the IRS, as a property. So, for your returns, it must be treated as such. Ensure you are aware of the tax implications, so you don't get any nasty surprises.

Chapter summary:

1. Trading in cryptocurrency is really just like trading in other fiat money currencies.
2. Research all aspects thoroughly before investing.
3. Find a safe, reliable exchange or broker to make your transactions.
4. Decide on the type of trading you want to do, long or short-term investments.
5. Seek expert advice to help you make the best choices.

6. Don't forget cryptocurrency is subject to the same taxation rules as other assets. Be aware of your obligations.

Your Quick Start Action step:

Visit the website Investopedia.com it has lots of great information on investing in cryptocurrencies.

Chapter 3:
How
Cryptocurrency
Works

Chapter 3: How Cryptocurrency Works

In this chapter, we will be looking at:

- The basics of how cryptocurrency actually works.
- How understanding the benefits of the inner workings can benefit you as an investor.
- The basic framework of cryptocurrency's functionality.

A cryptocurrency is a digitally generated computer currency that can be made secure by using cryptography. Cryptocurrency Coins, once generated, are stored in digital wallets that are protected with a key or passcode.

Coins can be sent from one wallet to another in a similar way to a direct bank transfer. Although cryptocurrency does not require a financial institution to act as the third-party intermediary. It is peer to peer, meaning it will go directly from one account to another with no middleman.

It is based on "Public Key Encryption," which is one of the aspects that makes it immune to the financial vagaries of individual countries or political regimes.

There are individual decentralized computers working on the network. These computers are known as nodes. These are run by private individuals who mine the network. They are referred to as "miners." The confirmation process for all transactions is called "Mining" and is done by the miners. It simply means that the transactions have been added to the public ledger. We will be looking at mining and blockchains in more detail in later chapters.

As with any career that's worth pursuing, reading as much as you can, learning the jargon and how the system really works in detail, can help you to avoid pitfalls. It can prevent you from making mistakes because you don't understand the processes fully. It is for this reason that it is essential to learn as much as you can about all aspects of cryptocurrency before you make any transactions.

Gather your information from a wide variety of sources. In this way, you can be pretty certain that before making any investment decisions you are armed with unbiased advice. That can help you make the best choices and help guide you to making your own well-informed decisions. If you do well, you may even consider an exciting new career as a cryptocurrency investor.

To recap:

1. Cryptocurrency is a digital, cryptographically secured form of financial asset in the form of a blockchain.
2. Transference of funds is (for the most part) anonymous, but at the same time publicly transparent.
3. Verification of the transfer is carried out by 'miners' computer systems that race each other to be the first to verify the transfer and thus set the transaction block in the blockchain.

4. Verification by way of public transparency gives you the ability to track the provenance of a coin all of the way back to the coins initial creation.

5. It is impossible to reverse a transaction, thus eliminating the chance of chargeback fraud.

6. It is de-centralized and essentially without borders. This can make the whole process of trading with companies in other countries less affected by fluctuating exchange rates.

Chapter summary:

1. Cryptocurrency is a financial asset that can be used for investment purposes.

2. It can be used for making financial transactions.

3. It is in general, decentralized and not under the control of any one country or political entity.

4. The coins are verifiably transparent to everyone, whilst maintaining the anonymity of the owner.

5. The provenance of a coin can be verified by anyone to ensure that the coin is not counterfeit.

Your quick start action step:

In order to learn more, try looking at websites like blockgeeks.com, Wikipedia.org, and YouTube.com. There is a great deal of information available online. But one thing to check is the date the information was uploaded, as only the most recent information is truly valid in this rapidly changing crypto world.

Chapter 4:
The
Cryptocurrency
Blockchain

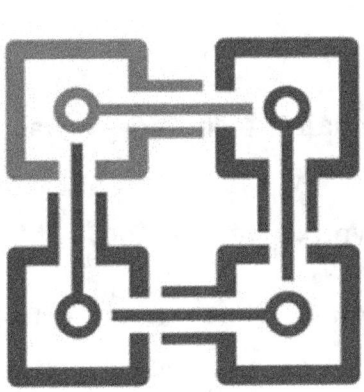

Blockchain

Chapter 4: The Cryptocurrency Blockchain

Satoshi Nakamoto was the inventor of the idea behind blockchain. It has moved on a great deal since this time, and the beauty of blockchain is that it allows digital information to be distributed, but it is not possible to copy it.

The blockchain technology was originally created for use with Bitcoin, but it is now used for other cryptocurrencies too.

It is assumed that the term blockchain originated from Satoshi Nakamoto referring to a chain of blocks in his original white paper. The first reference to the term blockchain seems to come from a conversation between Hal Finney and Satoshi on November 9, 2008. The term is likely to have been brought into daily use when the two words were joined to make the term blockchain.

Although not all cryptocurrencies work using blockchain technology, the majority do.

Blockchain is now being used for a far wider range of things than just cryptocurrency. The principles behind it are proving to be beneficial in many different industries. By understanding the basics of blockchain, what it is and how it works it can allow you to understand the wide range of benefits it offers.

1. **Reduced Transaction Costs** – As it is decentralized there is no need for a 3rd party clearing house, so overheads and fees are eliminated.

2. **Security** – The cryptographic safeguards within the blockchain make it very secure for all your transactions.

3. **Transparency** – Everyone can see what's on the blockchain because anyone can access the information on a computer. This severely limits the risk of corruption.

4. **Availability** – The system works by 1000's of different computers, known as Nodes, being linked to it. This means that even if some of the nodes leave, or stop functioning for any reason, that

there will still always be others available to guarantee the functionality of the system.

5. **Reliability** – The traditional method for maintaining databases was disorganized and susceptible to errors, corruption, and loss of information. Data sharing was difficult, and often only one user could update the database at a time. With blockchain, this is no longer the case. New data created by anyone with access to the system is first verified and then updated every few minutes. This adds new blocks of data to the chain. This data is viewable to everyone, but the encrypted parts are not visible to anyone, keeping your personal data safe.

6. **Speed** – Due to the speed of the blockchain verification process it has had a dramatic effect on cutting down the time it takes to get transactions verified, reconciled and cleared. This happens within a matter of minutes.

This is why blockchain technology is so interesting to so many organizations, including banks and financial institutions.

Information stored on a blockchain ledger is openly shared. It forms a database that is accessible to all on the Internet network. The benefits of this are that the information isn't just held in one place, like on a single server. It's held on all computers connected to the network known as nodes. This makes it effectively a globally distributed database of information. This also allows the records held on the ledger to be easily verifiable by members of the public. Because it exists in multiple places and hasn't got one centralized version, it's virtually impossible for a hacker to corrupt.

Traditional accounts and money movement are held and recorded on a banks central computer server. In order for changes to be made to an individual account, that account has to be blocked while the account is updated and money moved either in or out. When the process is finished, the account is unblocked, and the two sides of the transaction can be seen within the individual two accounts. This is how almost all databases work at the present time, with only a very few exceptions. The blockchain ledger works differently, as anyone can access it at any time and make their own transactions on it. But in order for these transactions to register as legitimate, they have to be verified using complex encryption protocols, by an unconnected 3rd party.

The blockchain network is self-auditing, it refreshes every 10 minutes and reconciles all transactions made. The group of transactions that this results in is called a block. The reason a block of information is so safe and incorruptible is because to alter any part of a block, would require the hacker to override the entire global network. It is theoretically possible, but in reality, is highly unlikely to happen.

As each new block of information gets added to the ledger, so the ledger builds chains of blocks. Each new block made contains some information from the previous block and a special number that ties it to that block. This is where the term blockchain comes from.

All the individual computers that are connected to the blockchain network are used to verify and relay the transactions being made. These individual computers are known as "nodes." These nodes (individual computers) create a powerful network, and each one is a separate administrator for the blockchain. Each node joins the blockchain network voluntarily, and this is why it is a decentralized network, as no single user is in charge. Nodes are incentivized to join the network in order to win cryptocurrency coins, this is called "mining" and is achieved by the individual "miner" solving complex mathematical puzzles.

Cryptocurrencies have been likened to telephone or fax machines. If only one person in the world owns one, then it is useless. But when people everywhere own them then the full potential can be realized.

Because the blockchain is a network of computers spanning the globe that have equal ability to manage the ledger (database), it means that the technology is decentralized, as it has no single authority in charge of it. It works purely on a peer to peer (user to user) basis.

At the current time, blockchain technology is very much in its infancy, but blockchain developers are in high demand as the uses for blockchain applications become apparent.

Currently, we rely on usernames and passwords in order to keep our digital information safe, and we know that these things are not that difficult for a hacker to compromise, so the application for a blockchain enhanced security is of much interest

We have all heard about organizations that have leaked or lost our personal information. If our information was decentralized by using blockchain, these incidents could no longer occur.

In the future, blockchain technology will enable far better methods of digital authentication, which has uses for many different industries. It will undoubtedly have a dramatic effect on business applications, and its influence will be seen in: Smart contracts, the sharing economy (think Uber and Air BnB), production markets, crowdfunding, file storage, governance, identity management, auditing of supply chains, intellectual property protection, neighborhood microgrids, anti-money-laundering, data management and registration of land titles, stock trading and many more besides. It really is the future.

The blockchain process simplified:

1. An update is made to the database. For cryptocurrency purposes, this would be a sale or purchase of crypto coins.
2. The information for the transaction, amount, details of seller and buyer are transmitted to all the nodes in an encrypted format.
3. The nodes check and verify the data.

4. A block is formed.

5. The block is uploaded to the ledger.

6. Every 10 minutes a new update occurs, adding an additional block of new data to the chain on the ledger

7. Each block contains elements from the block that preceded it. This ensures that the block sequence cannot be altered, as the blocks would not match up.

Chapter summary:

1. Blockchain was created by Satoshi Nakamoto and described in his white paper.

2. The first application for the use of blockchain was Bitcoin transactions.

3. Blockchains popularity is growing in many industries due to its low cost, security, transparency, reliability, and speed.

4. Blockchains work by adding new blocks of data onto a ledger. As more blocks are added, they are linked together, thus forming a chain of blocks or blockchain.

Your quick start action step:

You can research this in more detail by looking at the many guides on the Internet. You can try looking at websites such as www.coindesk.com and search the article called "How does blockchain technology work?".

Chapter 5: Different Cryptocurrencies and Picking the Right One

Chapter 5: Different Cryptocurrencies and Picking the Right One

Every day new cryptocurrencies come onto the market. At the time of writing there are well over a 1000 and exactly where the number will stop is unknown.

Many have been created just to jump on the bandwagon and will never be worth anything. Many will quickly disappear. But some, the select few, those using the best blockchain technology and backed up with real worth and a good team, will endure and are likely to continue to grow. But it's as well to keep in mind that this is a very volatile market, where big gains and big losses happen all the time.

The problem with so many new cryptocurrencies coming onto the market is that it's difficult to know which ones are going to make the best investment choice.

I cannot predict for you which are going to be the very best cryptocurrencies to invest in because no one knows exactly what the market is going to do. But this is information on the main players at the moment.

Bitcoin: Traded as (BTC). This was the first ever cryptocurrency. The concept for Bitcoin was created by someone calling themselves Satoshi Nakomoto, an unknown person. Nakomoto mined over 1 million coins prior to their launch in 2009 at a price of $0.008 per coin. Their value has subsequently risen to make them the most valuable coin in the world to date. They use the original blockchain technology and encryption safeguards.

Ethereum: Trades as (ETH). A fast-growing cryptocurrency which saw huge gains in 2017. It was conceived by Vatalik Buterin, a Russian born cryptocurrency researcher, and programmer. 11.9 million Ethereum coins, known as "ether" were pre-mined before the launch on June 30, 2015.

Litecoin: Traded as (LTC). Conceived by Charlie Lee, who was a former employee of Google, were launched on October 13, 2011. It uses the same blockchain technologies like Bitcoin but has a faster trading time.

Ripple: Traded (XRP). First conceived by Ryan Fugger in 2004. It began life as Opencoin but changed its name to Ripple on October 6, 2015. Then in September 2016 Ripple announced they had interest in the founding of their newly formed Global Payments Steering Group GPSG from banks including The Royal Bank of Canada, Bank of America, Union Credit, Santander, Westpac Banking Corporation and Standard Chartered. Today their Ripple protocol is being used by many worldwide banks and American Express.

When deciding which cryptocurrency you would like to invest in, it is essential to do your homework. It's a highly volatile market, where you can win and lose large amounts of money.

When looking for a coin that can gain significantly in value, don't just look at the coins price and the percentage at which it has been growing, also look at the coins market cap.

Also, look at the company background and the developers of that currency. Ensure that you like what you read and that the developers are a serious concern, with a strong team behind them.

Take a look at their website. Make sure it looks professional and is well written and that their information makes sense.

Look up the members of their development team where possible, and ensure they are experienced.

- If you can, try using their software and see if it works well
- The currency will have a whitepaper, read it and see if you like what you read
- See if you can find any mention of the currency having any security issues and if those issues have been addressed
- See if the main cryptocurrency brokers and exchanges deal in the currency. If they don't try to find out why

Chapter summary:

1. New cryptocurrencies are being created daily.
2. Some have legitimate reasons for creation, and many others do not, only back ones that do.
3. Some of the most popular coins at the moment include Bitcoin, Ethereum, Litecoin, and Ripple.
4. Check the background of a coin thoroughly before investing in it.
5. Check the circulating supply of a coin is not too high before investing in it.
6. Check the brokers and exchanges to ensure the coin is readily available. If it isn't find out why.

Your quick start action step:

By using the steps outlined in this chapter, find a coin you believe would be worth investing in. Then either try a small investment in it out or simply watch it for an extended period to see if your investment would have been a good one. You could do this for several different cryptocurrencies if you want to.

Chapter 6: Making your First Cryptocurrency Transaction

Chapter 6: Making your First Cryptocurrency Transaction

If you have never done it before, buying your first cryptocurrency can seem rather confusing and a little daunting. Once you understand what you need and how it is done, you will soon find that in reality it really isn't that difficult.

By now you should have chosen which cryptocurrency you want to buy (how to do this was detailed in Chapter 5). In order to buy any kind of cryptocurrency, you will simply need a reliable exchange or broker such as Coinbase (a full list of exchanges can be found on coinmarketcap.com), and a digital wallet (digital wallets are fully explained in chapter 7).

Make sure you check that the exchange you choose is a reliable - one that has not suffered any problems from hackers or unexplained loses. Check out feedback scores and what people say about the reliability of the exchange before using it.

Some exchanges have limits, and all have fees,

so make sure you are aware of what they are first.

These are the basic steps to making a cryptocurrency transaction:

1. Decide which cryptocurrency you want to buy and the amount you want to spend.
2. Chose the exchange you want to use.
3. Sign up for the exchange you want to use. Exchanges often only deal in certain cryptocurrencies, and only some exchanges will allow you to buy cryptocurrency with fiat money (regular dollars/pounds/euros, etc.), by using a credit or debit card or by making a bank transfer to complete the transaction.
4. A lot of the newer cryptocurrencies cannot be purchased on exchanges that will take fiat money, only on exchanges that will allow you to sell one type of cryptocurrency in order to purchase another. This is why they are called exchanges. You could, for example, use

Coinbase to purchase some Ethereum or bitcoin using your fiat money and then use that cryptocurrency on another exchange who sells your chosen coin to purchase it.

5. To join exchanges, you will require an identification document such as a passport or driver's license (if you don't then question that exchanges trustworthiness).

6. Follow the steps shown on the exchange's website to set up your account and to buy your chosen cryptocurrency. These are generally fairly easy to follow but do vary between exchanges.

7. You won't want to leave your cryptocurrency at the exchange for long, as it makes it vulnerable. You should transfer it to a personal wallet as soon as possible.

Bitcoin can also be purchased at a bitcoin ATM cash machine. These can be found at locations all over the world, and there are many different types. They all vary slightly in the way they operate. As an example, this is how one of the most popular machines found in the US works:

1. Press where it says "Buy Bitcoins."
2. You will be asked to provide your mobile telephone number by typing it in.
3. You will receive a validation code on your mobile phone, which you will need to enter.
4. You will be asked to scan your fingerprint.
5. You will be asked to select which coin you wish to purchase, and some machines sell other cryptocurrencies beside Bitcoin.
6. You will be asked to scan your wallet or to generate a new one.
7. If you have a wallet scan it.
8. Insert cash bills into the machine.
9. Press send.
10. You will get a printed receipt.

Selling cryptocurrency is done in the same way.

Again, different exchanges have different limits and different fees for transactions, so check them out. You will need your wallet so you can enter your private key when required

during the transaction. Make sure that your chosen exchange does crypto to fiat transactions and again simply follow the instructions on their website. If you want to use a Bitcoin ATM, then you will need your wallet and phone to make the transaction. ATM's have different withdrawal limits, so make sure you know what they are in advance.

It is likely as using cryptocurrency becomes more popular for day to day transactions that more ATM's will appear. Then more places will allow you to use your coins to make payments for goods and services.

This is what happens in a very simplified example of a cryptocurrency transaction:

1. (A) wants to buy cryptocurrency from (B)
2. (B) requires two pieces of information from (A) in order to do the transaction. (B) needs his private key (security code), from his wallet and (A) needs to provide her public key (a security code) from her wallet.
3. Once the required keys are in place, the transaction is uploaded to the cryptocurrencies' network, and the transaction is verified and added to the public ledger.
4. (A) receives the cryptocurrency into her account.

Chapter summary:

1. To make a cryptocurrency transaction find a trustworthy exchange or locate a cryptocurrency ATM.
2. Make sure they support the cryptocurrency you want to buy or sell.

3. Ensure you have your identification document, mobile phone and digital wallet (if you have one).
4. Follow the instructions given to make your transaction.

Your quick start action step:

Now you can try buying your first cryptocurrency coins or look at websites such as Coinbase for more information.

Chapter 7:
Storing
Cryptocurrencies

Chapter 7: Storing Cryptocurrencies

As I have mentioned previously mentioned a "wallet" is used to store cryptocurrency. This is pretty self-explanatory and simply refers to a way of keeping your cryptocurrency data safe and secure.

The cryptocurrency is not itself physically stored in the wallet. It is stored in the public ledger. When you buy currency, a private key is written onto the ledger so that only the person with that key can access and spend the currency associated with it.

If you want to actively trade in cryptocurrencies, it will probably be necessary for you to retain some of your coin at your chosen exchange. This will allow you to make trades quickly. The problem with keeping your coin in these exchanges or in online wallets is that it can leave you open to being hacked. It is also not unheard of for exchanges to just cease trading overnight. This is why it is far more advisable to put your coin into a personal wallet of which you have full control.

This method of keeping your coins is called "cold storage," as the coins are effectively taken offline and are no longer classed as "hot."

What are the best and worst storage options?

Home PC, Tablet or Smartphone - Some cryptocurrencies can only be stored on a computer or other electronic devices that can be connected to the Internet, such as a tablet or smartphone. But these are not, in reality, a good place to store your bitcoin. The reason for this is that they can crash, get a virus or computers can be fried by power surges on the grid. Have you ever dropped your phone down the toilet, or put it into the washing machine, or left it on the roof of your car, etc.? For these reasons, it is better to choose a different option.

If you have to store your coins on a computer, then consider buying a very cheap laptop or a refurbished one that has been professionally wiped. Then you can use it for the sole purpose of storing your coins. It then only has to be connected to the Internet and power outlet when you want to make transactions and is far less likely to be infected by viruses or hacked.

- **Desktop wallets**: There are many different desktop wallets available to download. They can only be accessed from one computer, the computer onto which they were originally downloaded.
- **Online wallets**: These can be used for any kind of computing device from any location. They work by using the cloud to store your private key information.
- **Mobile wallets**: Simply download an app to your smartphone. They are useful as they are so transportable.

Digital Hardware Wallets - These are special devices created for the sole purpose of storing cryptocurrency. These devices usually take on the appearance of a memory stick with a USB connection. There are several on the market, try looking for them on Amazon. The wallet you ultimately chose will depend on which currency you are going to store, as they are currency specific, so be sure you buy a wallet designed to store the currency you're buying. These wallets can be purchased cheaply and easily at online retailers.

The good thing about these hardware wallets is that they are simply plugged into your computer, and it is quick and simple to access your funds using a PIN code or security phrase. If your wallet is lost or stolen the information in it cannot be accessed. Some wallets give you the option to backup your information to an online account. You can also record your key by writing it down as a backup.

The problem with a hardware wallet is that like computers they can still be prone to power surges, water, hacking when connected to an online computer and loss. If you use cloud backup, then that can also be hacked. It can be a good idea to get a wallet that's water-resistant too.

Paper Wallets - This is currently the most secure method for cold storage due to them being completely offline. The right kind of paper wallet to use is one that is created by a special piece of software that prints the information required (public and private keys) onto special paper. They usually include QR codes so you can scan the keys rather than have to type them out. The problem with typing them out is that you are liable to make an error and that could potentially cost you a lot of money.

A lot of the software for paper wallets allows you to hide the private key. Or you can buy special tape that is tamper resistant and lets you tell if anyone has tried to look at your key.

You can purchase the software for paper wallets from the Internet. They usually also sell the tamper-proof tape. Before purchasing ensure you check out the security of the software generator. It's possible for an unscrupulous person to sell a wallet generator that covertly sends them your private key. With this key, they would be able to steal all the currency on your wallet by transferring it to their own. For this reason, it's important to research them online first thoroughly.

The best thing about paper wallets is that they are not subject to hacking or power surges and cannot get viruses. It's also easy to have multiple wallets, so you don't keep all your currency in one place, but equally, one wallet is able to store as much currency as you want to put on it.

No storage method is perfect, and even paper wallets have downsides. Essentially, they are bearer bonds. This means that whoever has possession of the wallet can claim ownership of the currency they contain. The reason for this is that the Key required to access funds stored on the wallet is actually printed on it. It is therefore essential if you decide to use paper wallets that you keep them somewhere safe, such as a safety deposit box.

You should use a specialist paper such as Terra Slate Lazer Copy Paper, which is water and rip-proof and readily available on Amazon. The reasons for this are pretty obvious, and regular paper can easily be destroyed by liquid, children, pets, fading, etc. Unfortunately, even the specialist papers can be destroyed by fire.

A laser printer should be used to print your wallet as laser print is waterproof. If possible try and use one that hasn't got a WiFi connection or a large internal memory. The reason for this is that this can lead to your wallet being hacked from the printer.

It is not possible to store all cryptocurrencies in a paper wallet, so ensure you know your options before purchasing your chosen cryptocurrency.

When buying Bitcoin, Ethereum or other currencies that support paper wallets, you simply use the software to transfer the information and print out your paper wallet. When you want to spend or withdraw your funds, again you use the software to scan the QR code printed on your paper wallet or enter the private key by typing it onto your computer. This is known as "Sweeping."

Brain Wallets - As you may expect, a brain wallet is a way of remembering a passcode. This is generally a phrase that allows you to access your cryptocurrency wallet. The usual format for this type of phrase is a random list of words

In order that no one else can access the information, you are supposed to remember the phrase without writing it down. You could, however, write it down in a way that no-one would recognize it as a passcode, by making each of the passcode words the second word of a sentence for example.

This option is not always available to you and has its own problems. If you forget your passcode, you will never be able to access your money. It is also not really a viable option if you're going to buy different currencies, which would be in separate wallets, or if you're going to keep you coins for many years. You could get a Cryptosteel, which is a metal device that lets you make a physical backup of the passcode. They are lockable, fireproof and waterproof.

Your cryptocurrency is only as good as the wallet you use. Because if your wallet is hacked, stolen, lost or forgotten, then your currency is gone forever.

To recap:

- **PC, tablet or smartphone** -Good points: readily accessible information. Bad points: Risk of hacking, loss, theft, damage, power surges
- **Digital hardware** – Good points: convenient, offline, easily transportable. Bad points: Risk of hacking when online, loss, theft or damage
- **Paper** – Good points: Totally offline so cannot be hacked. Bad points: Loss, theft or damage.
- **Brain** – Good points: Totally offline so cannot be hacked. Bad points: Can be forgotten.

Chapter summary:

1. A "wallet" is a method of storing your cryptocurrency key, so you are able to access your coins in order to spend them.
2. Hot storage – keeping your personal key information online.

3. Cold storage – keeping your personal key information offline.
4. Different types of wallet, have their own pros and cons.

Your quick start action step:

Investigate some of the step by step wallet making tutorials that can be found on sites such as:

www.coindesk.com/information/paper-wallet-tutorial/

www.buybitcoinworldwide.com/wallets/set-up/

Chapter 8: Investing in Cryptocurrency

Chapter 8: Investing in Cryptocurrency

Cryptocurrency investing really just means using cryptocurrencies as a form of investment. But what exactly is an investment? It's something that you purchase in the hope that over time it will become more valuable, so when you sell it, you make money. With cryptocurrency it is purchasing your chosen brand of coins, be it Bitcoin, Ethereum, LiteCoin, etc. in the hope that they will appreciate in value. If they do, you can sell them at a profit and make money.

When Bitcoin was first launched back in 2010, it took a long time for people to become interested in it and realize its potential. To begin with, only a few people could see just how much potential it might have. Many people now believe that for the first time ever, there's a chance for the world to have a single world currency in the not too distant future. When people finally started to realize this, they began to invest fiat money into buying Bitcoin, and the price of Bitcoin subsequently skyrocketed. For the lucky ones who purchased Bitcoin in the early days and have held onto it long-term, they have made vast fortunes from their investment.

Due to the success of Bitcoin, it didn't take long before other people started jumping onto the bandwagon too. It wasn't just Bitcoin as a currency that they saw potential in, but the bitcoin encryption platform and blockchain technology. This was because it totally changed the way people started looking at money. The cryptocurrencies themselves are only a small part of the story. In order for any of them to be successful in the long term, it is wise to remember that it's what's behind them that matters. This is really what you are investing in.

Understanding what to look for when choosing which cryptocurrency to invest in is vital to any chance of success. Here we will look at other things you must keep in mind when looking for the best investment opportunities.

- Learn how to pick the best currencies to invest in from the 1000's of choices now available.
- Learn what, other than the price and market value makes a cryptocurrency a good investment.
- Learn how holding onto your currency for the long term is often the best investment.

Choosing your investment currency wisely

Let's take for example one of the newcomers – Ripple, which is currently in the number 2 spot, behind Bitcoin and just ahead of Ethereum.

Many of the different digital currencies lack a clear purpose. Some are used to store value or for the purchase of goods. But their creation did not have any specific purpose in mind. The ones that do are the ones that stand the best chance of succeeding and gaining the most value in the future.

Ripple is different to Bitcoin, and it isn't a true decentralized currency. This is because al ripple coin was pre-mined before its public launch and a large quantity of Ripple coin XRP is held by the company in escrow. It was designed specifically to make international banking transactions much faster and most importantly a lot cheaper. The Ripple protocol has already been adopted by credit card giant American Express and banks such as Santander, Royal Bank of Canada and many more. As the benefits of the Ripple protocol continue to be proven, it is expected that other big names such as Visa and Mastercard may also join.

Based on the above you may think that Ripple would be a fantastic investment, and you could well be right, the two main problems with Ripple are that it has a huge market share and this will inevitably always keep its price low. But also, as the coins being held in escrow are released onto the market, they will dull the price.

Reason for being - Other cryptocurrencies have different reasons for being because when it all started, it was quickly seen that Bitcoins blockchain technology could be used for other applications. Among other things the tracking and storing of all kinds of important data, including legal, medical and financial information.

A lot of cryptocurrencies have no reason for being at all, other than people are trying to get in on the party. These have no real chance of ever being successful and will quickly disappear, as they have no worth behind them.

What use do they have? - When you have looked into what is behind a particular cryptocurrency, the next question you need to try and answer is: Is what they are selling useful? Will it be easy to use? Will it require no specialist knowledge by the end user? The answers all need to be yes. Yes, it will be useful. Yes, it will be easy to use. Yes, no specialist knowledge will be necessary. It's the same TV set analogy – you don't need to know how your

TV produces the images in order to watch it.

The team - The other thing to look at is how long the team behind it have been working on it. If the team only started working on the project a few months prior to launch, then the product is not a properly formed idea and won't have the protocols to back it up. You need to look for teams that have been working on their product for a good amount of time and really believe that their product has long-term use and value. This ensures you can be confident you know they have a real passion for it and want it to be a great product. It is these reasons why careful research is an essential part when it comes to making a choice over which currencies to back. It is impossible to say which will succeed and which will fail, because it is simply unknown and because new ones are appearing every day that could be better.

To find out more about specific currencies and what's behind them, visit their websites. Read the white paper on their product (it is likely to be written in geek, but you should get some of the ideas). Then you can make the best choices.

Market cap v coin price - It's easy to get swept away by looking at which coins have made the biggest profits in the past few weeks. Rather than only focusing on the price and the profits the coin has made, look instead at the market cap.

What exactly is a market cap? Basically, it means the total amount of fiat money (dollars, pounds, euros, etc.) currently invested into the cryptocurrency it is referring to.

Let us take for example Bitcoin. Let's say that its value today is $2000 and then the circulating supply was increased from 18.5 million coins to 185 million coins. This would cause the value of the coin to fall to $200. If you raised the circulating supply to 185 billion the value would fall to just $0.2. The amount of money invested in Bitcoin would still be the same, but its value would be severely diminished.

This is one of the concerns with Ripple coins. Because Ripple holds so many in escrow, if they were to dump them onto the exchange it would cripple the price of the coins and make them completely worthless.

Coins cannot be compared to just looking at their price or the amount of profit or loss they have made on the market. The only true way to compare coins potential value against each other is to compare their market cap.

If 2 coins have the same market cap value, but one of them has a lower coin price than the other, then the one with the lower coin price is generally, the better long-term investment.

By looking on coinmarketcap.com, you can view coins by their market cap from largest to smallest

The long-term - If you made an investment into a cryptocurrency (and had done all your homework as outlined above well), and in the first year it increased in price by an amazing $100 or $1000 dollars, you may well be tempted to cash it in. However, as Bitcoin demonstrated, it is easy to be swayed by media opinion. When Bitcoin rose in price from

$1,000 to $4,500, the media predicted that the "bubble" would burst and that the currency would soon see huge losses in value. This prompted many people to sell their coins. In reality, that's not what happened, and Bitcoin's value continued to rise. The moral of the story being, don't always listen to the media. Try to stick it out for the longer term if you are brave enough to do so.

Listen to the Internet chatter - There are many sites and forums where you will see regular information about different cryptocurrencies. Look out for the ones that a lot of people are predicting will do well. The likelihood is, that if a lot of people are of the same opinion and can give good reasons for their belief, that they could well be right. Make sure to do your own research too though.

It is also a good way to find out if a currency you have researched for yourself has any flaws that you didn't discover yourself.

Finding the right broker and secure wallet - As previously discussed in chapter 6.

The final thing you need to do is find a reputable exchange to use when buying and selling your coins. Just as important, is to ensure your currency is protected in a safe "cold" wallet to avoid theft, damage or loss.

To recap, things to check before investing:

- **Purpose** – Does the cryptocurrency you want to invest in have a clear and meaningful purpose?
- **Use** – Does the currency have a practical use or feature that will make it more popular than others?
- **Individuality** – Is it unique?
- **Team** – Is the team behind the creation and development of the currency strong with top professionals from their field?
- **Market Cap** – Has the currency got a good market cap, giving it greater potential value?
- **Long-term** – Are you willing to weather the ups and downs that ALL currencies experience for the long term,

allowing your investment to reach its full potential?

- **Listen** – Is the Internet chatter about the currency you are interested in positive?
- **Broker/Wallet** – Is your chosen broker reliable and trustworthy with no history of loss? Is your wallet safe?

Remember cryptocurrency is a very volatile thing, where huge losses, as well as gains, can and often do happen. Honestly, a lot is just down to pure dumb luck.

Chapter summary:

1. Investing in cryptocurrency means buying your chosen brand of coin in the hope it will increase in value over time, in order for you to make a profit.

2. It took several years for people to appreciate the potential of digital currency. Today it is a huge market, worth billions of dollars.

3. Many coins have seen huge rises in value, while many others vanish into obscurity.

4. Chose your investment coins wisely, always check Purpose, use, individuality, design and management team, market cap, your long-term commitment, Internet chatter, broker and wallet security.

Your quick start action step:

If you are interested in investing into cryptocurrency, you will need to put aside the time to do the research necessary to make the right choices. Try and schedule that time into your calendar today.

Chapter 9:
How to Avoid
Investing
Mistakes in
Cryptocurrency

Chapter 9: How to Avoid Investing Mistakes in Cryptocurrency

As you have read through the chapters in this book, you will have seen what you should and should not do. As an overall reminder, you will find here a list of common mistakes people make. This is not an exhaustive list, so be sure you are always careful and do your due diligence before making any transactions.

1. **Not doing your research** – If you don't fully investigate the cryptocurrency you invest in, as outlined in chapter 5, you cannot complain if that currency fails.

2. **Mining** – Don't think that going out and buying your own crypto mining rig and starting her up is going to make you rich. Mining requires massive amounts of electricity, and really successful rigs require huge amounts of computing power. So, unless you can afford a rig costing many 1000's of dollars and can

then hook it up to a solar farm, it is probably not worth it. If mining is something that interests you and you'd like to give it a go without the hefty price tags, you can join a consortium and take out a stake in a large mining setup. These can be found by doing online searches. But beware, there are many crooks out there, so ensure you check them out thoroughly before handing over any money.

3. **Holding your nerve** – As I highlighted in the previous chapter, you may need to be brave and look at holding onto your coins for the long-term. It is easy to get spooked into making rash decisions to sell your coins when they experience a crash. Hold your nerve, don't be tempted to sell. Instead, give them time to mature and reach their full potential.

4. **Private Keys** – This is one of the biggest mistakes rookie investors make, not knowing their private keys.

Hundreds of millions of dollars have simply evaporated into thin air because people didn't remove their wallet service offline to somewhere safe, an offline wallet. If you don't do this you don't have full control and your coins can be stolen or the information lost.

5. **Online communities** – There are dozens of online crypto communities. They are collectively hugely knowledgeable. Their combined knowledge and expertise can really help guide you into making sound choices, but more importantly, help you to avoid making costly mistakes! You can also post questions on the forums to get helpful answers about anything you are unsure about.

6. **Wrong wallet** – Another easy mistake to make is to accidentally try to put newly purchased currency onto the wrong wallet. Wallets are generally designed to hold only one currency. If you hold several currencies on different

wallets, it can be easy to mix up your wallets and try to put new coins on the wrong one. Doing this will result in disaster and the loss of your coins, so beware! Some wallets do support more than one currency, by they don't support them all, so check first.

7. **Hard copies** – Always keep hard copies of all your passwords and private keys etc. Print them off and store them somewhere really safe. If you lose these you have lost the currency they pertain to.

8. **Exchanges** – Ensure the exchanges you choose, have two-factor authentication. This will help safeguard your purchases. When you receive your restoration code, don't just leave it on your phone, write it down somewhere safe. If your phone is lost, stolen or replaced, you will have lost your restoration code too and may not be able to access the currency you have on the exchange.

9. **Criminals** – Due to the amount of money involved in cryptocurrency, it has inevitably attracted a large amount of criminal interest. Do your best to check things out in all aspects before making any decisions. Keep in mind at all time that people are out to steal your money and take all precautions you can to safeguard it.

If you follow the steps above you can look forward to a fun and hopefully rewarding time investing in cryptocurrency. If not, then you could potentially lose any money you invest in it.

Chapter summary:

1. Always do your own full and thorough research.
2. Be aware that mining isn't a cheap and easy way to earn cryptocurrency. Consider joining a mining consortium.
3. Remember "Fortune favors the brave."
4. Look for your private keys and passwords! Keep a hard copy offline.

5. Get help and information from online communities to avoid making costly mistakes.

6. Make sure you use the right wallet when buying currency.

7. Investigate the exchanges well before using them.

8. Be aware that criminals always want to steal your money, so be careful who you trust and take precautions to safeguard yourself.

Your quick start action step:

When you next go to buy cryptocurrency, remind yourself of the mistakes to avoid first, so you don't inadvertently make them yourself.

Chapter 10: Trading in Cryptocurrency

Chapter 10: Trading in Cryptocurrency

What is cryptocurrency trading? Just like traditional stock market trading, cryptocurrency trading involves the short term buying and selling of cryptocurrency. Quite possibly the most famous 'trade' will forever be the Hanyecz pizza trade in 2010, which involved the exchange of 10,000 bitcoins for two pizzas, each one of those pizzas being worth over $80,000,000 at the time of writing this guide!

Comparing trading and investing; investing in the acquisition of cryptocurrency and holding it for an extended period of time. The purpose of which is for the currency to grow in value over that time. It requires the investor to weather the downtrends, anticipating that the value will once more increase and grow to exceed its loss.

Trading, on the other hand, is looking at the relatively short-term ownership of a cryptocurrency with the aim of making a faster (and generally smaller) profit. To do this, it is necessary to buy when the price is low and sell when it has increased in value and reached your desired profit margin. On the whole, trying to avoid the ownership during any downtrend.

There are various styles of trading: Position Trading, Swing Trading, Day Trading and Scalp Trading. These styles of trading refer to the length of time that elapses between buying and selling and can range from months and years to merely a few seconds or minutes. Profit can also be achieved by 'selling short' which would involve borrowing cryptocurrency when it is at a high price, selling it and then buying it back when it has lowered in value.

Understanding how trading in cryptocurrency works is important. Short term gains are possible to achieve, by following the trends closely and taking a more active role in how you manage your cryptocurrency investments. It requires you to check values and trends daily actively. This allows you to sell for the higher and more immediate profits rather than weathering out the ride of the long-term peaks and troughs.

The benefits of learning cryptocurrency trading

- You are able to take advantage of the short-term highs and lows in the market
- You can take control over the money that you have invested in cryptocurrency
- More frequent short-term profits can be achieved
- Faster returns

The basic steps on how to trade in cryptocurrency

1. You will need cryptocurrency wallets for the currencies you want to trade in.
2. You will need to join a cryptocurrency exchange such as Coinbase.
3. Start by trading the more well-known coins such as Ethereum and Bitcoin.

4. Consider joining another currency exchange in order to trade coins that are not traded on Coinbase.
5. Keep a very close eye on trends.
6. Remember, you don't have to buy whole coins.
7. Follow the blogs and news concerning cryptocurrency.
8. Keep a record of all transactions for tax purposes.
9. Fees are payable on transactions.
10. Be aware that not all cryptocurrencies are the same and that as well as huge gains, huge losses are also possible.

Chapter summary:

We have looked at the broad outline concerning trading in cryptocurrency. As a recap here are the salient points to remember.

1. Trading allows you to put your money in cryptocurrency for the short term in order to take advantage of price fluctuations.

2. In order to trade you need a cryptocurrency wallet and to join an exchange.

3. Take an active interest in the trends and decide what kind of trading you are comfortable with.

4. Start by trading coins that are more established until you are comfortable with this market.

5. Be aware of the tax implications.

Your quick start action step:

Make time to fully research trading further. Ensure you look into the currencies, exchanges and the communities in order to make the best choices. If you want to take trading seriously, you will need to have the time available to look at your position in detail on a daily basis. Try to schedule time in your diary now in order to make a start and look at how you could fit it into your life on a regular basis.

Chapter 11:
Risk
Management
Essentials for
Cryptocurrency
Investing

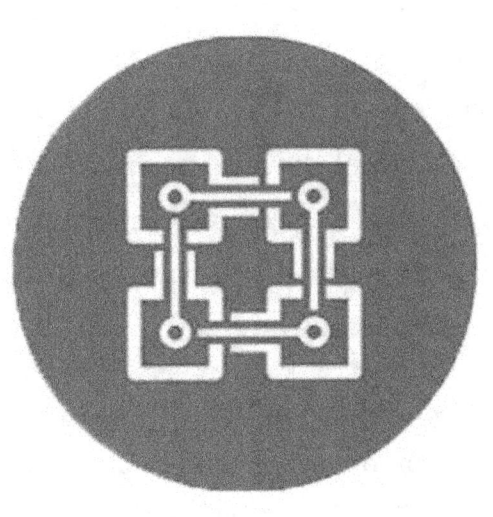

Chapter 11: Risk Management Essentials for Cryptocurrency Investing

What is "Risk Management"? It is simply the term used in the financial world to describe the identification, understanding, and analysis of the financial risks. Then to process, avoid, limit or accept them. As part of investing or trading cryptocurrency, you should attempt to find and predict potential downturns and decide if you should take action or no action when they occur. By doing this, you can potentially avoid making large losses.

If there is a lot of chatter on the media and in the forums about a particular currency about to take a massive downturn, and it is backed up with good reasons for why this might be the case, it could be worth cashing in that currency before the downturn happens. Then if it does, you won't lose out. However, sometimes chatter is just that, chatter, and either nothing happens, or the currency actually continued to increase in value (as has been seen with Bitcoin and Ethereum). Or also like Bitcoin and Ethereum the coins do suffer large losses only to make them up again with even larger gains. I didn't say this was going to be easy!

The benefits of knowing about and implementing risk management are it can help you to:

- Understand the market better
- Predict when some big change is going to occur
- Avoid big losses
- Predict coins that may be about to make large gains

How risk management is done

1. Risk is inherent with all investment, in order to keep abreast of what is going on you need to keep a close eye out. To do this, you can use certain websites such as cryptocoinnews.com and altcointoday.com.

2. It is also a good idea to regularly visit the cryptocurrencies' own website for news, good or bad.

3. Keep an eye on the Internet chatter, the information being released by worldwide media and on forums.

4. Watch how your coins are faring in the market by looking at websites such as coinmarketcap.com

5. Never over invest. You must only ever invest money you can afford to lose without it affecting your life in any way.

Chapter summary:

1. Risk management means assessing and responding to potential risks.

2. It can help you to make informed choices.

3. It helps you to stay one step ahead.

4. Use websites, news media, and forms to keep up with the latest information.

5. Keep a close eye on the markets.

6. Never invest more than you can afford to lose.

Your quick start action step:

Try implementing one of the above steps. I would suggest either looking at websites, news media, and forums or watching the markets.

Bonus Chapter: Bitcoin Mining Essentials: The Benefits and How It Works

BONUS Chapter: Cryptocurrency Mining Essentials: The Benefits and how it Works

Mining; what is it and how does it work? In the context of cryptocurrency, it is the verification of transactions and inclusion within the public ledger, the blockchain. It is also the method for the creation and release of new coins.

When the cryptocurrency bitcoin came into being, so did a new transaction verification process called Blockchain. The verification of transactions is carried out by 'miners' discovering new blocks that have been created from the various transactions that have been grouped together. This is done with a computer, known as a mining rig, which can perform very complex mathematical computations, necessary for mining.

Mining a block is purposefully difficult to do. This is to ensure that the number of transactions being mined enters the ledger at a steady rate.

As more miners join the network, the rate at which the blocks are being created naturally increases. As the rate increases the difficulty of the mathematical algorithms that must also be solved increases. This helps limit block creation and ensures that it is continuing at a constant rate. Blocks released that do not meet the required level of difficulty are rejected by other miners on the network and so fail the confirmation process.

Miners who successfully complete the complex computations necessary are rewarded for their efforts by winning coins and are also given a small transaction fee.

Miners compete with one another to be the first to solve the difficult computational problem. The first to solve it received the bonus coins and the transaction fee. When Bitcoin started up, the rewards were 50 coins which by 2014 had halved to 25 coins. In the early days, mining could be achieved from a regular desktop computer with a decent graphics card.

By 2013, specialist hardware was introduced, and an efficient mining rig needs to have a very fast graphics card and powerful CPU (central processing unit). The profitable, competitive mining can only be done today with the latest "Application-Specific Integrated Circuits" otherwise know as ASICs

It is not necessary to understand how mining is done in order to buy and sell cryptocurrency, just like it isn't necessary to know how your television works in order to watch it. It is, however, comforting to know the process. To understand the safeguards it provides and speed at which transactions can be made.

If you are interested in mining cryptocurrency for yourself, then you will need to obtain specialist hardware. This hardware can be very expensive, although you can buy mining rigs second hand. Miners also need A mining software package, membership in an online 'mining pool,' membership of online currency exchange and a coin wallet in which to keep any earnings. Mining uses huge amounts of power running 24/7, and this makes it very expensive to do.

Keep in mind that the more popular a particular cryptocurrency becomes, the less cost-effective the process becomes. As a hobby, mining can give you a return on your own infrastructure expenditure. However, it is not going to provide you with an income sufficient to quit your job.

Another alternative is to join a mining consortium, details about these can be found online.

If you do decide to 'mine,' please do your research on your coin or coins of choice as 'scam currencies' could cost you dearly.

This is how a transaction is done from start to finish:

1. Your request to buy units of cryptocurrency
2. The request is received by the seller of the currency

3. The seller requests your public key shown on your cryptocurrency wallet (if you have one, if not a wallet is created).

4. The seller then uses their private key to release the currency to your wallet.

5. An alert is sent to the cryptocurrencies miners that are on the network around the world.

6. The miners on the network verify that the seller has sufficient currency to make payment to you.

7. Miners then race to compile the data from your pending transaction and other unrecorded transactions that have been made, plus the most recent block of transactions that were recorded into the public ledger and a random number called a nonce.

8. The miner then includes a mathematical function called a hash. This produces a cryptographic fingerprint that makes the block of transactions unique and verifiable.

9. The hashed block of transactions must have an unspecified number of zeros at the beginning of it. Its nonce will have the correct number of zeros, so it is necessary for the miner to keep trying different amounts until hitting on the correct one. This process is called proof of work.

10. When the miner finally finds the hash with the correct number of zeros, it is announced to the rest of the network.

11. Other miners then communicate to show acceptance, before then trying to find the next block so that the whole mining process starts again.

12. The miner who found the correct hash for the block is rewarded with coins and the transaction fee.

13. The newly confirmed block is published into the public ledger.

14. Within a matter of minutes, you receive notification that the cryptocurrency coins you purchased have been assigned to you.

15. You will then receive several more notifications as the transaction is embedded into subsequent blocks.

Chapter summary:

1. For the majority of cryptocurrencies, mining is an integral cog in the machine. Although not all cryptocurrencies use mining or blockchain.
2. Mining is responsible for the verification of the transactions carried out.
3. Miners are rewarded for their efforts with a currency that has been created as a byproduct of the mining process. (Note not all currencies can be mined).
4. In order to successfully mine, dedicated and specialist hardware and software is required.
5. It is a highly competitive process.
6. It produces the public ledger, the blockchain which makes the verification of a coin's validity transparent and verifiable.

7. Setting up a mining rig and buying the software can be expensive.

Your quick start action step:

As with all aspects of cryptocurrency, before deciding to embark on a new career as a miner, further reading and research are essential. This will help you better understand the costs and the processes involved. It will also show you the realistic potential return you can make on your investment. There are many sites on the Internet from which you can gather more detailed information by doing a simple search with one of the main search engines such as Google. One site you can look at is iqmining.com.

Conclusion

Thank you for owning this book! I hope you found it to be of value, easy to understand and informative.

The next step to learning more about this interesting topic is to do further research in the areas highlighted within the book. By doing this, you will be able to make informed choices on which are the best cryptocurrencies to invest in and, avoid making costly mistakes.

Finally, if you have enjoyed the book and found it to be of value. I would be most appreciative if you would leave a review for it on Amazon. Your help here would be greatly appreciated.

Thank you and good luck!

About the Author

Gavin S. Finney is a Bitcoin and cryptocurrency investor who have written several books on the subject.

As a successful investor, he then got interested in digital currency and Bitcoin during its early stages, but got frustrated learning the technical topic.

Gavin wanted a method that he could easily learn from in order to understand all about digital currency and how to make money out of it. He soon discovered a teaching series online that made him learn faster and better.

Applying the same approach, Gavin successfully made his first digital currency transaction which triggered the start of his digital currency success.

With the books that he writes on the subject

matter, he aims to provide readers with great value and in the hopes that they too can experience the same success investing and making money from cryptocurrency.

Glossary of Terms

Blockchain: A decentralized, digital, public ledger of all transactions made.

Circulating supply: Total number of coins available in any specified cryptocurrency.

Cryptography: A method to store and transmit data in a form that only its intended recipients can read and process. Cryptography protects data from theft or alteration and is used for user authentication.

Decentralized: Moving control from one central authority to many individuals.

Digital signature: A digital code, generated and authenticated by public key encryption). Attached to an electronically transmitted document to verify its contents and the sender's identity.

Digital Wallet: A form of storing the digital signature and reference codes pertaining to an owner's cryptocurrency.

Double spending: A form of theft where one set of coins is spent in more than one transaction.

Fiat money: Paper currency, Dollars, Pounds, Euros, etc.

Hashing: A method of encrypting data.

Market cap: Total value of any given cryptocurrency.

Nodes: Individual computers situated on the network.

Peer-to-Peer: Person to person, or wallet to wallet.

www.ingramcontent.com/pod-product-compliance
Lightning Source LLC
Chambersburg PA
CBHW071315220526
45468CB00001B/388